WAITING FOR THE TROUT TO SPEAK

Poems by
Irene Blair Honeycutt

Irene Blair Honeycutt

Charlotte, North Carolina

Copyright © 2002 by Irene Blair Honeycutt

Cover image based on the photo, "river of grass,"
by Irene Blair Honeycutt
Cover design by M. Scott Douglass
Back cover photo by Eike Diebold

Library of Congress Cataloging-in-Publication Data

Honeycutt, Irene Blair.
　Waiting for the trout to speak : poems and prose poems / by Irene Blair Honeycutt.
　　　p. cm.
　ISBN 0-9708972-3-5
　1. Nature—Poetry. I. Title.

PS3558.O467 W35 2002
811'.54—dc21
　　　　　　　　　　　2001006478

ISBN 0-9708972-3-5

Published by
Novello Festival Press
an imprint of the Public Library of Charlotte and Mecklenburg County
310 North Tryon Street
Charlotte, NC 28202

Produced and designed by
Main Street Rag Publishing Company
PO Box 691621
Charlotte, NC 28227-7028
www.MainStreetRag.com

Acknowledgments

I am grateful to the editors of the following publications in which these poems—some of which have been slightly revised—originally appeared.

Asheville Poetry Review: "Eclipse '92"
The Bear's Tale: "Blessing"
Independence Boulevard: "Bernstein," "It Is Snowing in Belfast, Maine"
The Lyricist: "On Meister Climbing the Fence in Spring"
Main Street Rag: "On the Museum Wall at Terezín, a Handkerchief," "Postcard to David," "The Rest of Our Lives"
Mount Olive Review: "After Seeing Liv Ullmann's *Sofie*"
Southern Poetry Review: "To Paint the Portrait of a Baby Bird"

Anthologies:

Earth and Soul, a bi-lingual anthology of North Carolina Poetry, Eds. Mikhail Bazankov (Kostroma), Sharon D. Ewing and Judy Hogan (Moncure, NC: Kostroma Book Publishing Project, 2001): "Driving Up 181 to Jonas Ridge"
No Hiding Place—Uncovering the Legacy of Charlotte-Area Writers, Eds. Frye Gaillard, Amy Rogers, and Robert Inman (Asheboro: Down Home Press, January 1999): "Boundary Waters"
The Sandburg-Livesay Award Anthology (Pittsburgh: UnMon America, 1999): "The Collector"
Trapping Time Between the Branches—An Anthology from Charlotte Poets, Eds. Don Carroll and Frye Gaillard (Charlotte: Public Library of Charlotte and Mecklenburg County, 1993): "The Courage of Turtles," "How Can I Stoop to Wash My Face in the Surprise?"

With much gratitude to the many friends who have encouraged this manuscript, including Joseph Bathanti, Janet Blair, Peggy Brooks, Vinny and Lynda Calabrese, Liz Carroll, Bessie Chronaki, Helen Copeland, Bud and Trudy Cox, Kevin Davis, Nancy Dorrier, Naomi Myles, Sheryl Willis Deutsch O'Neal, Tim Peeler, Diana Pinckney, Missy Sawyer, Rebecca Schenck, Gilda Morina Syverson, Mary Ann Thomas, Leslie Tompkins, and Mary Wilmer.

Special thanks to Keith Flynn and Ione "Tootsie" O'Hara for their invaluable critiques of the manuscript. And my deepest thanks to Maureen Ryan Griffin who believed in this book over the years of its development and who devoted countless hours in its service.

I want to always honor my teachers—those who remain unnamed but whom I remember with much love and respect; and two, to whom I owe so much: my high school English teacher, Rosanne Hartwell (*in memoriam*); and my college English professor, Margaret English Livermore.

My gratitude also extends to Amy Rogers and to Frye Gaillard for their dedication to excellence and for their hard work on behalf of our community of writers.

For my brothers
Ralph, Ronnie and Ray Blair

And to the "child in us that yearns—longs—to just once more take the long walk down Superior, to Beaver Street for the Sunday School Hour, from Lowell Avenue 2584."

Contents

Preface   ix
Introduction   xi

Part I   Steep Ravine

To Paint the Portrait of a Baby Bird   3
Boundary Waters   4
The Escape, Honolulu   6
Because the Leaves   8
The Sage   9
Dry Rain   10
The Collector   11
"The Courage of Turtles"   12
Signature Spider   13
Eclipse '92   14
The Raptor Center   16
each pond...a prayer   17
Steep Ravine   19
Blessing   20

Part II   A time for moons

A Time for Moons   23
Little Towns   24
After Seeing Liv Ullmann's *Sofie*   25
The Barber Shop   27
Good Friday   29
Farewell, after Bach's *St. Matthew Passion*   30
Imagining Winter Whole   31
Early October   32
The Rest of Our Lives   33
St. Francis of Assisi   34
Walking by the Vltava   35
Embroidering, 1949   37
On the Museum Wall at Terezín, a Handkerchief   38
The Village of Argostoli   39
Postcard to David   40
O   41

Part III   All the way home through the dark

Driving Up 181 to Jonas Ridge   45
Waiting for the Trout to Speak   46
One World   48
All the Way Home Through the Dark   49
Ruth   50
Bernstein   52
Inventory   54
Map   55
The Path to Alligator Pond   56
Leaving, Another Summer   58
It Is Snowing in Belfast, Maine   59
Stroupie, One Autumn   60
The Train Man   61
How Can I Stoop to Wash My Face in the Surprise?   64
2584   65
Meditation in January   66
Stone Offerings   68
On Meister Climbing the Fence in Spring   69
The Poem Might Begin With Mornings   70

Notes   73
About the Author   75

Preface

~~~~~

I remember a Saturday afternoon in 1991 when I was leading a small group of writers on a journaling retreat at Upper Creek Falls. After we had hiked to the waterfalls and eaten our lunch on the rocks, I removed a poetry book from my knapsack and read aloud a poem by Raymond Carver entitled "The Trestle." We each wrote a response in our journals to the question: What would I like to do the way my father did?

~~~~~

Many times I have reflected on what I recorded in my journal that day. My father had died of cancer. Because he was such a quiet, shy man, I regretted that I had not known him better. Writing in my journal while sitting close to the motion of water, I began a process that helped to heal memories and led me to discover my father anew. I truly learned that death does not end a relationship. Here is a portion of what I wrote that spring:

My father loved to fish. I never went fishing with him until he'd built his boat house after Mama'd died and he'd remarried. I marveled at the father I'd never known. . . . I stretch out on the hot rock and now I see the boat house rising at the edge of the lake . . . the silky green lily pads floating near the motor blades . . . I see the fish scales in the sink . . . the fillet knife glistens beside the small bream Daddy caught this morning while I was still sleeping . . . I see him holding the bait, his eyes squinting in the sun, his fingers patiently threading the anchor's eye. I see him making the perfect cast, clearing the cypress stumps. He sits there for hours—patient like that—the way he sat in silence alone at night on the screened porch, smoking his Lucky Strikes . . . . I see him quiet and when he turns, sitting like that in the boat, reeling in the trout, when he turns, he asks for the first time if I ever hear from Mama. I am sitting in the boat with my back to him, my throat so tight the words barely come . . . . The next time he will ask about her will be on his deathbed. There he will come out of the coma and ask: "When did Laura die? I mean, exactly what time did she die?" And then he will go to meet her . . . .

~~~~~

It is important to remember that we are not just writing about the past. For the past, as William Faulkner has so eloquently written, is never past, but always with us. Alfred, Lord Tennyson in his poem "Ulysses," expressed a similar thought when he wrote: "I am a part of all that I have met." Writing leads us to connect with the present. It takes us deeper into an exploration of the paradox of time past and time present. At the heart of writing is the opportunity to express who we are *in the moment*. When we immerse ourselves in the process of writing, being totally present to the life unfolding on the page, writing becomes a journey—a great adventure—filled with unexpected insights. It provides a map to our inner selves. The way is often mysterious.

~~~~~

On some level I'm still trying to answer the question: What would I like to do the way my father did? I think it has something to do with living out my life with, well, I'm still writing into the answer. As Rilke implored in his *Letters to a Young Poet*, we must "be patient toward all that is unsolved in [our hearts] and . . . try to love the *questions themselves* like locked rooms and like books that are written in a very foreign tongue. . . And the point is, to live everything. *Live* the questions now. Perhaps [we] will then gradually, without noticing it, live along some distant day into the answer."

~~~~~

The journal entry about my father took me deeper into my own creativity, moving me in and out of different memories. Past became present as I began to write a poem about my father. During the process I searched through old family photographs and found one of him sitting in a rowboat. At the time, I thought that the poem began with that photograph. However, I later realized that the poem actually had begun long before. It was anchored in childhood memories and brought to the surface through journaling. The act of journaling freed me to write the poem, "Waiting for the Trout to Speak."

~~~~~

I invite you, the reader, to contemplate the metaphor.

<div style="text-align:right">Irene Blair Honeycutt
June 11, 2001</div>

Introduction

It's a privilege to be writing this introduction—a privilege for me personally and on behalf of all the other writers and readers in Charlotte who have benefited so greatly from Irene Blair Honeycutt's presence in our midst.

I heard of Irene Honeycutt numerous times before I met her. "You should take one of Irene's poetry classes," my friend Gilda Morina Syverson had told me, on more than one occasion. "It'll help your writing so much." "Irene is the most wonderful teacher!" my friend Katherine McIntyre had exclaimed repeatedly in her soft, Southern syllables. "You'll just love her!"

You were right, Gilda. You were right, Katherine. Irene is a gifted teacher, unsparing in her commitment to excellence. She inspires; she pushes and prods the best out of her students. Under her tutelage, many of us have gone on to teach classes and publish poetry collections of our own—a tribute to her talent.

Irene is also a generous mentor and a passionate advocate for what literature provides. I've seen first-hand, in the eleven plus years I've known and come to love her, how dedicated she is to creating opportunities not only for her students, but for the whole community to grow as writers and readers, and to grow spiritually as well. Through individual readings, lectures and workshops, and through the CPCC Literary Festival, which she founded ten years ago, Irene has worked tirelessly to bring a stream of wonderful writers to Charlotte—Natalie Goldberg, Stephen Dunn, Mary Oliver, Peter Meinke, Patricia Hampl, Miroslav Holub, Anne Lamott, Robert Haas, Li-Young Lee and David Whyte—to name just a few. In the appreciation and enjoyment of all this, it is easy to lose sight of one important fact—Irene Blair Honeycutt, in addition to her other talents, is a fine poet in her own right.

I was lucky enough to be in that small group of writers at Upper Creek Falls on the Saturday afternoon in 1991 that Irene mentions in her Preface. The depth of feeling and the richness of the images in her writing touched us all. We, along with her, left that day *with the memory/of water, the sound/ of it falling off boulders/and swirling around slabs/of granite, sliding off flat/ rocks into hollow/beckoning pools...*("Waiting for the Trout to Speak"). Some years later, Irene shared with me this manuscript, centered in this title poem. I loved it when I first read it, moved by the aching loveliness of such words as *How, then, can I stoop to wash my face in the surprise/of blackberry blossoms white above the rosy dianthus?* ("How Can I Stoop to Wash My Face in the Surprise?") and *The birds flurried; the leaves shook amid the clatter. He clapped again and laughed, orchestrating their dark rapture* ("All the Way Home Through the Dark"). Her love of other poets is present throughout in poems such as "One World," her elegant spinning off from Elizabeth Bishop's classic poem "One Art"; and "On Meister Climbing the Fence in Spring," after Richard Eberhart.

Many of these poems are masterpieces of chiaroscuro: lit by fire ("The Collector") and candlelight ("Boundary Waters"); by porch light ("Leaving,

Another Summer") and lamplight: *I am drawn to the yellow glow/of those rooms—as if we once had lived there...* ("It is Snowing in Belfast, Maine"); even by flashlight: *and the shepherds shouting through the fog, stroking the leaves of the olive trees with their flashlights' beams* ...("The Village of Argostoli").

Many are sketches of sun and color: *how to/capture this/shade of red—/not the red of wound,/nor red of plum skin./Closer to flesh/of strawberry/ freshly bitten, juice/glistening* ("To Paint the Portrait of a Baby Bird"); *Something/about the way afternoon sun sweeps/over the white house with the green/shutters, ...light glancing off the/bundles of hay in the fields and the way/the leaves are filling up with light before/autumn slips in...* ("Little Towns"). It's remarkable, as a reader, to be present to such brilliant light in the midst of heart-wrenching moments, as in "The Barber Shop"—while the speaker is facing her brother's cancer, she is remembering his blond curls falling at his first haircut: *They fell so gently to the gray tile floor,/and lay there till there was a heap/softer than the buttercups we'd picked that summer,/ the shiny strands glinting in the sun, golden....*

And many more moments glow with the moon, that universal symbol of the cyclical nature of our lives, of hope and renewal. I'll leave you to discover these on your own, except to mention one of my favorite poems in this book, "Driving up 181 to Jonas Ridge," in which the moon's *December face radiates gilt/enough to paint the ridges stiff/in gold leaf./It pours itself out and still/has more to spare....*

Reading this luminous collection, which encompasses an unflinching acceptance of loss and grief, I thought of poet Alan Shapiro's saying that our songs of lament are really songs of praise, because we lament what we hold most dear. There is so much that Irene Blair Honeycutt holds dear, not just in her own life but in the lives of so many others, from Dr. Anna Polartova, executed in Berlin in 1943 ("On the Museum Wall at Terezín, a Handkerchief") to the bear starving in Sarajevo ("Because the Leaves"); from the sacks of corpses lining the roads in Bosnia to a dead finch on the deck, *its feet curled tight/as lady's-slippers;/delicate weight,/a small stone in the palm;/the eyes/black stars, the light out* ("Dry Rain"). We, the readers, are blessed to stand, *For a moment...amid the soft wet/silence of snow/falling/...feast...on the/...branches/ of the cherry tree each braced/to catch the weight of snow/and hold with/ infinite grace/what settles there* ("Meditation in January").

I've been waiting for a while, not only for the trout to speak, but also for this collection to be found by the right publisher. How perfect that this has turned out to be Novello Festival Press, right here in the community to which Irene has contributed so greatly. Bravo!

Maureen Ryan Griffin – June 11, 2001
When the Leaves Are in the Water

I. Steep Ravine

> —*Nature not a book, but a performance, a high old culture*
>
> *Ever-fresh events*
> *scraped out, rubbed out, and used, used, again*
>
> —Gary Snyder, "Ripples on the Surface"

TO PAINT THE PORTRAIT OF A BABY BIRD
after Jacques Prévert

First
paint it
terrified
fallen
into dead leaves
eyes
not formed yet
unable to see
the dangers
outside the nest.

Then
paint something
from another
world
perhaps you
bending
to scoop it
into your
palm.

Lean
the canvas
against
the dogwood
in your backyard.
Allow the ache
as you marvel
at the openness
of the tiny life
that stretches
its beak
for food
you do not
have.

Try
to paint
the mouth
as you would
the center
of a flower
after rain,

this mouth
more delicate
than porcelain
waiting for you
to fill it
with a splash
of color.

That's a problem,
too: how to
capture this
shade of red—
not the red of wound,
nor red of plum skin.
Closer to flesh
of strawberry
freshly bitten, juice
glistening.

And how to paint
your fear
of failing?
Imagine yourself
moving lightly
across the lawn
of canvas,
lifting

yourself
with the bird.
Part the ligustrum
and let the tip
of your brush
release it
into the nest.

Paint your sadness
flying away
as you pull back
empty,
closing the bush
with one quick
stroke.

And now
you must relinquish
any haste and listen
as the father cardinal
clicks messages
from a world
you can never
inhabit

   though
watching him dart
from limb to limb
you may learn
motion of ascent
motion of descent
from fence
into shrub.
Then you can aim
for the promise

that dangles like the sacrificial worm
                      in his beak.
Finish by painting the leaves where he flew
                  trembling   as if in wind

BOUNDARY WATERS

To know the dark, go dark.
              —Wendell Berry

1. What Is It I Have Come Here for?

   I haven't seen the sun, the moon
   or a winter star all week. I light
   a candle, read a poem at the edge
   of the woods, close my eyes and wait
   before the trek to the center of the lake.
   Going into the night without a light
   I ease my way over ice and discover
   that darkness grows inside the dark.
   Slowly, the island comes into view,
   blossoms over frozen water.

2. Night Walking

   No language for it:
   How the darkness lights itself.
   No language for night seeing,
   for darker than dark. Walking
   on ice, I circle the island, search
   for wolf prints at the shoreline—
   surprised when I find them:
   How soft they are,
   floured with snow.

3. Not Knowing What to Listen for

>   I wait.
>   At the end of my flashlight's beam,
>   the bold blue stare of a husky.
>   The wolf never howls this close
>   to the dogs.
>
>   Suddenly
>   white light
>   between my ears—
>   the sound of ice breaking
>   beneath me.

4. Winter Rain

>   Outside the winter rain
>   pelts the frozen lake.
>   Beneath the ice
>   waters are always flowing.
>   Somewhere a wolf pads over snow,
>   while the huskies rest,
>   curled into beds of straw.
>   I lie in my sleeping bag
>   on the floor, thinking
>   of the leaflike tracks I carved today
>   snowshoeing to the island
>   bushwhacking through spruce.
>
>   And how the wind on the other side
>   stopped howling.

THE ESCAPE, HONOLULU

One afternoon inside the circus tent,
things happening as usual, an elephant balked.
When the trainer prodded and shouted,
this largest of mammals went berserk,
    swung her trunk in defiance,

knocked the trainer to the ground,
then stomped, crushing him while children
watched from the stands, licking
cotton candy from their hands.
    A hush fell when they realized . . .

Then screams shook the canvas walls
as the elephant fled, running into the crowded
street, terrorizing drivers who'd grown up
watching King Kong climb to the top
    of the Empire State Building.

The elephant's mate, perhaps drawn
by the scent of the sea, took a different route,
lunged into the ocean and began swimming
as if trying to get back to Africa.
  After repeated shots, a rifleman's bullets

felled the one running with the herd
of traffic. Crumpling to the ground,
    what was she remembering?

    It was like a suicide pact,
witnesses stated, wondering later
about her sad eyes, the drooping folds of skin.
TV reruns showed sessions of the trainer
    beating the elephant
with a rod to break her spirit,
ripping with a hook what looked like leather.

Elephants remember everything,
a commentator reported. *And love to walk,*
often traveling fifty miles per day.

But that's on home ground where they bathe
  in sand, not here where they march
  in silence from railroad cars to fairgrounds
  or where in cages, legs chained they sleep,
lying on concrete, perhaps dreaming
of wild fields, rivers,
  leaves for burying their dead.

BECAUSE THE LEAVES

are falling

in Sarajevo

and no longer

can hide

the zoo keeper

who fears

sniper's fire

and cannot

get close enough

to toss

meat between

the bars

of the cage,

the bear rummages

through the leaves

licks its dry claws

while the world watches

over TV screens

its starving

THE SAGE

The sun like a hot coal
burns into the west

                    From the center of the earth
                     the Great Blue surprises,
                            lifts,
                      presses the wind,
                wings bluer than I've ever seen

                        How patiently he
                  flies across the field and lights
              before beginning his solitary stroll
                    through brown grasses

Purposeful in his aloneness

   he moves like some mythical sage
                          roaming his dominion
                                        thinking things through

Beside a leafless tree
he waits
as if he has arrived
deliberately early
for an appointment

                        Hedrawstheduskclose

DRY RAIN

A few weeks of spring here
and cherry blossoms color the ground.

On the morning news, in Bosnia
sacks of corpses line the roads.

How to honor the faint disturbance?
—the finch upside down on the deck,

its feet curled tight
as lady's-slippers;

delicate weight,
a small stone in the palm;

the eyes,
black stars, the light out.

I fashion a gesture

line the grave
with honeysuckle leaves,

let the earth sift
between my fingers

THE COLLECTOR
for Trudy

Sourwood dangles
orange seeds
from barest branch
as if to tempt
her gaze away
from heather's yield
of blossoms white
as starlight.
Rooted in rocks
atop the ridge
Sawbriar leans
green and slick
across the trail,
tears hikers' flesh,
licks its thorns
along a line
of blood.
Where rivers once
pushed mountains up
November strolls,
shaking black pods
of coins,
plucks each tree.
The leaves tremble
like old men's hands
in wind
reaching for fire.

"THE COURAGE OF TURTLES"
—Edward Hoagland

I know what he means.
I saw one once
when I was riding my bike
across a field.
It brought me low
to see the window
someone had blasted
through its dome.
My blood slowed
as I gazed at the moist
labyrinth of its secret
temple, my hands poised
in a dilemma,
the ranger station
just a mile back.

I think I lifted
it gently enough,
set it on its stubby
columns into high grasses,
pointed in the right direction.

I left it there.

Days later when I rode by
I caught its essence.
I poked among the weeds a while,
found nothing
but the wind and some sense
of lost momentum.

I pedaled slowly
towards the woods.
A solitary parade.

SIGNATURE SPIDER

Summer ended
and already the spider
  with yellow stripes has
  moved into the porch
  light and spins twin webs
    strung like silken
  hammocks hung sideways
    through the evening
Chopin and rain and
    now and then
    my dog and I
    at the window
      watching
the spider   weaving
    its signature
    at the center
and though I don't write
your name because it hurts
    still to do that
I think of the message
  you sent today after
    months of distance
saying you were wondering
   if my hair moves
  when the raindrops
     touch it
    late into night
  the webs tremble

ECLIPSE '92

Two a.m.
The fog so dense the foghorns
sound blind, the harbor lights only
a flicker in memory. "Come quickly,"
you say. "The moon is back!"
I hurry from the bed, not wanting
to miss that first moment
when earth's shadow nudges the moon
before erasing it from the sky.
Through binoculars the moon looks
fragile as chalk dust. If I rubbed it,
it would powder my hand.

Huddled beneath blankets, we sip
raspberry tea beside the spruce
that grows so close to the cottage
it tickles our arms every time
we climb the steps.
In this early morning hour it droops,
drips dew onto our toes.
A gull squalls as buoys clang
eternal warnings to whatever
is coming in from the deep.

Yesterday I saw the whales.
Twenty-five miles from shore,
near Mt. Desert Rock, blowing
and gasping.
Pursued by marine biologists
in an orange raft,
the whales rose and fell—
brave, glistening monuments.
Standing in the scientists' boat,
after all these years of longing
to see them, I watched the harpoon
skim the sea foam, wondered
what they felt when it struck.
They flattened the waves and sank,
leaving only their whale prints
on the ocean for me to photograph
and some blubber in the test tubes.

Again the moon is back.
Dark clouds sail past like
Odysseus eluding the sirens' calls.
The buoys' clangs grow shrill.
"What are you thinking of?"
 you ask.

How to say
that I would like to sing to the whales.
To the ones that will beach
or thrust themselves before the gunner
to protect a mate.

Beneath this cleansing moon
the waters shift and churn.

THE RAPTOR CENTER

                I never meant to see them—
tied to those hoops
                            leather bands hugging their legs
shiny talons clutching fake bark.
                      Out for a Sunday hike,
I'd stumbled upon this sideshow at the edge of the woods.

            it happens this way now and then
                  (I wanted to say)
          i feel your breathing inside my own

          Drawn by the park ranger's lecture, I moved
into the crowd and listened to each one's plight.
The barn owl turned its snowy
                          heart-shaped face away;
the barred owl refused to close
                          its bright eyes.
And the great horned hooted:
                      who-do-you-think-you-are?

           I had somewhere else to be, certainly,
not gawking at these creatures

              blinded by someone's bullet
              wounded by a car's bumper

when they, perhaps reeking of wild skunk, swooped down
              for mice at the side of the road.

     and now
        in dreams
            do they sift the darkness
                    through tilted wings?

A slight wind sprang up and blew a light white feather
        from the screech owl's breast
                        past my shoulder.
     I reached to catch it.
              Let it drift . . .

EACH POND...A PRAYER
—Mary Oliver

Early this morning I watch the mallards skid
  onto the pond
    the tufts of blue
      beneath their wings
        glistening

Towards the edge a mother is guiding
  her ducklings where ripples slide
    between the filigree of roots
      still holding
        the willow

Now the little ones are practicing
  calisthenics over root
    and rock
      over one lonely
        tree stump

      learning to peck
        the water's surface
          for survival

And here I stand on the pier
  close to the green swirl
    where air bubbles speak
      of life hidden there
      and soon

      a brown duck emerges
        for breath

Listening

    as twelve form a circle
      at the pond's center
        how can I not believe

      in yet another
        language beyond
          our knowing?

And just
  when I think of leaving
    a turtle appears
      its head protruding
        like a floating twig

      but the ducks are not fooled
      and sound
        cacophonous warnings

So even here
  with the sun
    barely risen
      and a fountain
        spurting life and movement

      the ancient themes insist
        on being noticed

And in the white oak
  a lone grackle
    contributes
      an awkward cry

STEEP RAVINE

Lying inside the sleeping bag spread out against the plank window bed, like a boat with no oars I drift off course into a sea of dreams where anemones adorn the sea floor and starfish float along the ocean sky— myriads of pinks, mauves, bronzes, purples, gold — where no human shadow bends over them.

~~~~~

And now to sit on the small rocks feeling the sun burning through my sweatshirt, hearing the rush of fresh rain water tumbling over rocks and the crest of ocean waves rising, the low rumble of waves rolling in....To see a few feet ahead where the rain has formed a quiet pool and where beyond the ocean roar the brown pelicans glide and fishing boats drag nets. Gigantic boulders perch at precarious angles on fragile limestone. How everything tilts, is in the process of shifting. Even we who pause and reflect have only to gaze at this marvel of sea—taste and hear it—to have our perspectives altered.

~~~~~

How the body shifts. I think of Baudelaire's poem about the tourists who, returning from a sea voyage, shouted *At last!* when they saw land; his own response being, *Already?* So it is. The ache too soon in the heel, the fragile ankle turning, the skin cancer growing near the left eye's tear duct.

A wide margin of clouds borders the horizon; the sea goes gray; the moment suspends itself like the hawk hovering above the cliffs the way a kite stiffens in the wind. Only a gull's squeal breaks the spell; then, once again, the grinding sea.

—Steep Ravine, California, July '97

BLESSING

The moon
moon turn
almost before
full its
climbs lonely
the pass
trunk across
of the
the stars.
loblolly White
pine, oaks
chasing hold
the up
raccoons their
away, arms.
slowing Dry
the leaves
world. whisper.
For We
a drive
moment in
it silence,
balances no
on need
fingers for
of headlights
pine before
sheaths the
for paved
one road
quick appears: the world we left behind

II. A time for moons

> *. . . the one road*
> *whitened in moonlight leads everywhere.*
>
> —Philip Levine, "Ask for Nothing"

A TIME FOR MOONS
for my niece

Her seventh summer
and Lorie is naming the sounds
she's heard on Jonas Ridge.
Last night she swore a bear
lumbered up Gingercake Road.
In her poem the dogs bark always
in the valley; fighting cocks crow,
tied to their cages; and only squirrels stir
up the red and yellow leaves.

She does not write of sounds
she heard when she and her brother
fell asleep staring at pineknots dark
as bats and witches.
The chestnut branch that scratched
the shingled roof entered
her nightmares and my own
when she woke me,
crying about a skeleton
clawing a hole through the screen
and dragging Ray from his bed.

She twists her lips,
bites the eraser, considers
rambling into the moon
that rises over the hill.
"The moon is scary,"
she says. "It don't sneak
up that way in Florida!"

There will come a time
for moons, I tell her, sinking
back into my dream
where my brother stands in front
of a harvest moon that is melting
into our backyard. Holding a book
he steps closer
as if to instruct me how to read
a life he is leaving,
the word *sister* caught within his stutter.

LITTLE TOWNS

Something about the blue house
on the corner of Grove Street
when I turn left at the traffic light
at Main in Lincolnton. Something
about the way afternoon sun sweeps
over the white house with the green
shutters, the way the light slides onto
the car seat and something about that
light on the gray peeling
off barns and light glancing
off bundles of hay in the fields
and the way the leaves are filling up
with light before October slips in.
                                            Light.
How it feels
    sweet and silent
        distant and cold.
                                            And me,
not wanting to let it go

AFTER SEEING LIV ULLMANN'S *SOFIE*

Over wonton soup and spring rolls
we labor to discuss the film.
I stammer around subjects,

gesture with my hands,
drop noodles into the bowl—
anything but try to explain

why I cried
or how I felt when the camera
focused on the daisies

where *Sofie* wrote at her desk
or how her father's eyes caressed
his wife's in the portrait—

how that aroused within me
a familiar ring of loss
so mixed with longing

over something as simple as a worn
quilt shaken out of the closet
for another season.

By the time the fortune cookies
arrive with tea, we are recalling scenes:
lovers tiptoeing around each other,

the children too enmeshed
by Jewish mothers; the listless way
Sofie's husband talked, walked, or read;

how his blue eyes stared vacantly
into hers; the hint of passion
that met with awkward fumblings:

the hand on the breast too soon,
the rush of lust thwarted in madness.
And all those birds in cages!

So many women trapped, knitting and singing,
until the blanket of death silenced
the dreams they concealed inside the books

they read and the letters they wrote.
*Risk means a willingness to live
in unfamiliar terrain.* This,

they never discussed. And neither do we.
Though I keep thinking about Jacob's refusal
to drink from the wild mountain—how this

bred a paralysis reflected in his feeble
smile. So that I cringed with Sofie when,
unexpectedly, he entered the bedroom,

feasted on her nakedness, then turned
into the beast she had to kill.
Near the film's end, seeing her framed

in the cliché of a photograph
and staring at a life once lived,
I remember how sometimes

I've caught myself not breathing,
so I inhaled deeply as if
I could recover lost time.

And now across from you,
I think of times when watching you
crossing the parking lot,

I've wanted to break through windows,
fly after you,
make love in the leaves.

THE BARBER SHOP

You were only three when Mama and I walked you
down McDuff Avenue to Mr. Davis's barber shop.
I touched the giant peppermint stick
mounted next to the door and hoped he'd give us
some real candy for coming. You sat stiff on the board
he'd placed over the arms of the black leather chair,
and I watched you clench the armrests,
your knuckles turning white as wishbones.

He tried to cheer you by patting Old Spice on your cheeks,
the way he did when Daddy got a shave along with a haircut;
but you fretted, anyway, and said it burned,
and each time his long silver scissors snipped a blond curl,
you sobbed and begged Mama not to let him do it again.
They fell so gently to the gray tile floor,
and lay there till there was a heap
softer than the buttercups we'd picked that summer,
the shiny strands glinting in the sun, golden
as the filaments the princess had spun
in that room where the king kept demanding more.

I didn't know it would hurt you so.
I kept watching the curls drop as if they, too,
might suddenly wail in protest.
Walking home, we licked vanilla ice cream.
I held your hand, and life went on as before
though everything had changed.

Years later, with your hair falling out in shocks,
we walk side by side, up and down the halls.
The nurse teases you not to speed with the I.V. monitor.
Your fingers are wrapped around the pole the way Hansel's
gripped the door of the witch's cage. Inching your way
along the corridor, past the elevator, you are learning
to walk again, building stamina for the happily-ever-after
ending the doctor doesn't believe in.

The other patients, bent on their beds, watch
as we pass their doors.
Though tempted to hold onto your arm, I don't
because you're the one out here walking,

giving it your "best shot," you say, setting a new
goal when we return to your room.
The nurse rolls the dinner cart towards the bed.
"Dinner's on me!" you grin,
asking for an extra plate.
We sit across from each other,
chewing tough roast beef.
I watch the drops of chemo crawl through the tube
and think of Grethel—
how she knew the Duck could only ferry them
over the water to the other side one at a time.

GOOD FRIDAY

At this odd hour before the alarm sounds I am down on my knees in the workroom searching the recycling bin. Page after page of old news I thumb through. Then I spot the photograph spread out on concrete. The paintbrush I'd cleaned and left to dry covers her face. I rub my hand over this woman to press the wrinkles out. Why did I discard her only to want her back? It is Good Friday, *Sarajevo's second Easter under siege.* Her face is rutted with centuries, eyes narrowed to keep her longing in check. Shrouded in black, she dares not lick her lips. The kerchief tied at her throat has knotted her voice. Standing in front of a booth at the open market, staring at a plucked chicken dangling from a string, she looks like a frozen winter day. With eggs and tulips priced at three dollars each, the chicken at $33, I wonder what she bought that day. Did the gray sky at her back burst into flame?

FAREWELL, AFTER BACH'S *ST. MATTHEW PASSION*
for Mary Nell Saunders, 1949-1993

> "When choirs under her direction performed the music of Johann Sebastian Bach, listeners felt they were present at the creation of a spiritual world...."
> —*The Charlotte Observer*

It plays all over again—
the night she lowered her head
and the music stopped
at 8:42.
The score had blurred
into darkness.
We imagined her backstage
and wished for the gift of her hands
when the audience sang the final hymn,
then waited for the choir in black
to answer back:
"O sacred head now wounded,
with grief and shame weighed down."
I counted myself lucky
among the crowd—somewhere
in between deaths.
It was not what we came for,
the ancient story made real
while tulips bloomed red at home.
The Resurrection Morning approaching,
I thought of the cardinal that pecked
bewildered at the patio door.
The stage curtain drawn back,
we saw ourselves reflected,
the stone rolled away.

IMAGINING WINTER WHOLE
for Peg

For weeks she'd turned the earth,
pleasured in the spade swiveling
into the depths she'd measured
before she dropped each bulb
into the hole, all the while
imagining spring—the garden
birthing yellows, reds, purples.
Still, her heart longed
for the deep snow
that had not fallen.
Brushing the soil from her hands
one day she saw herself far
away, rocking by the fireside
in a cabin, remembering snow-
shoeing, dog sledding, skiing
across a frozen lake.
She didn't want to miss
that memory she'd imagined
standing there, so she dreamed
her way to somewhere else—
her life too smooth and white
without footprints. She saw
the snow she would cut into.
It would happen beneath
icy stars: a winter whole.

EARLY OCTOBER
for Ronnie

Picture us walking
along a sidewalk,
past the morning papers
rolled like bread
and tucked into boxes,
the clear October light
on our bare arms
warming our hair
and sliding across
park benches.

Picture us walking
along a grassy path
to the school
close to the woods,
our puppy nosing
the green acorns
that fell last night.

Picture us walking,
touching red berries
on dogwood trees,
the dog sniffing white
mold on a thick
brown leaf.

And now I am walking
across leaves,
hearing them break
and listening
to the bite
of a buzz saw
blocks away,
my thoughts
on you
in another city,

your voice
over the phone
telling me
of the tumor
in your spine,
lymphoma
hiding

within your cells.
Last night
shotgun blasts
took the grackles
by surprise
scattered them

                through space
      hundreds   their sense of place
                                            lost
            hyphenating the sky—

whirling   amassofconfusion   Imagine them

      circling   like that   unable

            to
                    light

THE REST OF OUR LIVES

"We've got the rest of our lives
to do that," she said,
as if the road were endless.
On the other end of the line
I swallowed my response
because in an hour I'd be leaving
for Greece.
Seems we're *always* just moving on
to something else.
Like playing hopscotch,
I told her once, only forgetting
to take time to pick up the glass.

En route
the light on the wing's tip pulses
as I stare into the void
thinking...*if its heartbeat quit,
this 767 in mid-air holding
us over the Atlantic*...but
I stop the thought.

Later I'll learn that when my friend called
to say goodbye her mother, newly engaged
at seventy-five, was planning her garden wedding.
And my brother at forty-seven was giving a nurse
100% cooperation when she stuck his flesh eight times,
trying to find the right place to insert the chemo tube.

"It's the needle that tried my patience,"
he tells me now, long distance. Untangling
the cord, I scramble for words to express
how amazed I am by his courage,
remembering how I was always the one
who played the Lone Ranger sending him
on a mission as Tonto to scout out
the dangers ahead.
All he wants for his birthday is some time
with me—just to drive somewhere, go
to a movie, maybe a short trip
to the Stephen Foster Memorial
to revisit our childhood.
"No cruise?" I prod.
"No cruise," he says,
his smile blossoming through the phone.

ST. FRANCIS OF ASSISI

The lime tree
holds
the silence
of the stars.
Above the hill
the moon
tilts,
pours
its orange glow
into the valley.
Smoke
curls
from the burning olive
bush.
Is this God's
handprint in the
leaf
and in the little
rivers
running across my
palm?

WALKING BY THE VLTAVA

Weathered rowboats inhabited by geese
rock in the river with Time
still eating the blue paint.
Weeping willows, as if lured,

rock in the river with Time
swimming green, bow in the wind.
Weeping willows, as if lured
by their reflections

swimming green, bow in the wind.
A fisherman dips his net
by their reflections
into a skimmering shadow.

A fisherman dips his net.
At the same moment, above the Charles Bridge,
into a skimmering shadow
an old woman leans out a window.

At the same moment, above the Charles Bridge,
her bony arms scraping the ledge,
an old woman leans out a window,
her eyes feasting on bread crumbs.

Her bony arms scrape the ledge.
A light bulb dangles from the ceiling.
Her eyes feast on bread crumbs.
Something draws me back.

A light bulb dangles from the ceiling.
I meander until
something draws me back
to the underground chapel.

I meander until
trying again for peace I return
to the underground chapel
of the Order of the Knights.

Trying again for peace I return
to the chapel of St. Francis
of the Order of the Knights
of the Cross with the Red Star.

In the chapel of St. Francis
I inhale the fragrance of ancient stone
at the Cross with the Red Star
as if it could permeate my bones.

I inhale the fragrance of ancient stone
as if all memory could rest here,
as if it could permeate my bones.
Yesterday, walking through the cemetery

as if all memory could rest there,
I searched for Kafka's grave.
Yesterday, walking through the cemetery
I heard the chestnut trees.

I searched for Kafka's grave.
Mound after mound where ivy flowed,
I heard the chestnut trees
dropping their thorny ornaments.

Mound after mound where ivy flowed,
I heard the tap-tap of a hammer and trees
dropping their thorny ornaments.
On one grave a man stood chiseling.

I heard the tap-tap of his hammer and trees,
and my body vibrated with Life.
On one grave a man stood chiseling
someone's name into marble.

And my body vibrated with Life
still eating the blue paint,
someone's name in marble,
weathered rowboats inhabited by geese.

EMBROIDERING, 1949

Mama's in the kitchen frying mullet
and boiling grits for supper. I'm sitting
on the sofa leaning into the lamp light,
embroidering by myself for the first time.
Mama pressed the wooden hoops
into place so there's not a wrinkle anywhere.
I like the way the cloth fits tight as a toy drum.
Every now and then the silver thimble slips
off my finger when I try to push the needle
through the linen. I take tiny stitches,
small as ants. I'm embroidering a red flower
with yellow seeds at the center.
If it's done right, Mama says when I finish
this piece she'll let me work on a blue bird.
I've seen the pattern.
He's singing on a tree limb,
so I'll get to use lots of pretty threads.
I want her to be happy.
The neighbors say Mama's work is the best.
When I grow up I'll have scarves and pillow
cases just like the ones she makes for them
with pink roses climbing over the corners
and lace around the edges that looks like snow
clinging

ON THE MUSEUM WALL AT TEREZÍN, A HANDKERCHIEF

> *Dr. Anna Polartova participated in the PWZ Activities representing the Women's National Council. She was executed in Berlin, 1/19/43. She embroidered the handkerchief for her nephew.*
> —text panel,
> Museum of the Terezín Ghetto

A red aster radiates
at the center.
In one corner a toy drum
awaits a tap.
From another
a rooster stretches its neck,
crows in bright yellow streaks.
On a border
the train puffs off track
and Tram No. 5 clamors
towards Old Town.
A rattle rests
beside an infant's bottle.
A clown laughs by himself.
The little black terrier
will never stop barking.

Still life:
red cherries,
cluster of grapes
on the counter,
one ripe banana . . .
Potato soup steams
in the bowl
with the silver spoon.

All
on white linen,
even the house
of memory
with chimney and gray
smoke curling off the edge

THE VILLAGE OF ARGOSTOLI

Why, years later, with ice covering the grass do I remember again that night in Argostoli when we walked out of the walled garden to listen to the church bells and heard instead sheep bells like rain falling in the fields? This morning, listening to Puccini and watching the red-bellied woodpecker hop up the pine—its cap ablaze with winter fire—I thought of how we stood close in the darkness where the narrow dirt path and the field met; how we leaned against a stone wall and held our breath and listened to the brass bells strapped to their necks. That is how we knew how far into the meadows they had roamed. For a long time we paused, and the village dogs began to bark before we saw the low shifting clouds of white and heard the bleating—the bells louder—and the shepherds shouting through the fog, stroking the leaves of the olive trees with their flashlights' beams. We allowed them that much privacy; for we turned soon to the sounds of our hiking boots mingling with those of other strangers, shuffling along the dusty path that wound to the center of the town. We sat on the steps in front of the church, gazing up at the steeple piercing those empty spaces among the stars and fell asleep waiting for the bells.

POSTCARD TO DAVID

Thought of you today—Cephalonia a blaze of color. Remembered your pink hibiscus, the parrots trapped between frames on the walls of your salon. Biked to the lighthouse along a trail that wound by the sea past laurel, orange poppies, jasmine. Startled when a peacock promenaded out of bamboo reeds onto the path. Last night, Angelina and I pedaled the winding streets after midnight. Crossing the low bridge where water lapped at our wheels, I could have spun off forever.

Her mother enticed me into the icy Ionian Sea.
I braved it but quickly hobbled back over beach stones to soft sand. I've discovered Greece never goes to sleep. The grandmother pushes open the garden gate for a late night visit at ten. If I wake at three, someone is always walking by. This morning it was Chrisula, the village misfit. I crept out of bed and watched through slanted shutters as she muttered at the moon, snatching bougainvillea petals and stuffing them between her breasts. Even I've let the craziness in. Or is it out? For one day around noon I stretched out on a park bench next to Chrisula's and snoozed without being arrested. *Zito!*

O

a lament for Beverly Suggs, 1924-1997

O
bitter-sweet moon
of March

I turn out the porch light
and step outside
my eyes blurring
in the dark

and all the while

you are climbing
slowly higher
and too soon will curve
around the corner

at four a.m. I rise from my bed
and gaze through the curtains
as you wind your path
over the neighbor's house

heading toward morning
you will be a pale breath
at dawn
when she wakes

and the nurses lift her
from the hospital bed
wheel her into the belly
of the medic plane

lying on a stretcher
like cargo she will fly
over the house on Ferncliff
over the homes of friends

over the parks
the fish camp by the river
over the schools where
she studied and taught

it will all converge
the life left
the one to come
and flying out of her life

watching the earth shift
beneath metal wings
as if all would dislodge
slide off the horizon

she will think of
her husband lost
to Alzheimer's and hope
that before she vanishes

into clouds
he might look up
and hear the roar
of her heart

    O

III. All the way home through the dark

How to speak. I believe that if a woman poet survives, if she sets out on that distance and arrives at the other end, then she has an obligation to tell as much as she knows of the ghosts within her, for they make up, in essence, her story as well.

—Eavan Boland, *Object Lessons*

DRIVING UP 181 TO JONAS RIDGE

The winter moon rises
full to brimming—
a gold-hammered icon
shimmering above the overlook
where generations have seen
the Brown Mountain Lights.
Its December face radiates gilt
enough to paint the ridges stiff
in gold leaf.
It pours itself out and still
has more to spare,
so spreads a Byzantine angel's
wing over Jonas Ridge.
When I drive past an ochre field
close to Joe Poore Road,
I want to stop, for someone
has decorated a weathered shed
with Christmas lights;
and the ancient moon,
having followed me up the mountain,
glows on the horizon of this simple farm.
I think of the magi following
their star
and have read that
in every icon the artist leaves
a space for the viewer's soul
to enter. Somehow I feel
I have often been in this scene
standing beside the road,
gazing across a field
at the moon brightening
the ashen sky.

WAITING FOR THE TROUT TO SPEAK

A stone glints
like a fisheye
caught by the sun.

I leave
with the memory
of water, the sound

of it falling off boulders
and swirling around slabs
of granite, sliding off flat

rocks into hollow
beckoning pools. It's
the forgotten memory
I keep fishing for,

one that swims so deep
I can never cast far enough,
even in dreams.

I've glimpsed it sinking
behind my father's gaze
when I stare at the photograph

of me on his knee
when I was two. The palm tree
at our backs seems to wave

goodbye... the way it did
when hurricanes swept
through in September

rushing my toy boats down the gutter.
Memory lost so far back
I can't even recall when

the conversations stopped
in our house.
A swift current swallows

those shy attempts at words
my father sometimes made
on the screened porch after supper,

the smoke from his Lucky Strike
trailing off into the smouldering dark.
This summer I framed a snapshot

I took of him the year before he died.
He looks content there—
sitting in the row boat

shrouded in silence
beside the lily pads
waiting for the trout to speak.

ONE WORLD

Our losses fall in love with one another.
Something lasts, will not be shorn by grief,
though we feel like a lamb from mother driven to the slaughter.

A new-born dream emerges from the darkest corner
of despair and all that was. Though bound by disbelief,
our losses fall in love with one another.

The droning spell of lost affection hovers over
each borrowed hope, each unhinged cry for relief.
Torn in two, we are like lamb and mother driven to the slaughter.

Sitting at scarred tables we watch the world re-order.
The wren constructs its dome of broken twig and ragged leaf
while our losses fall in love with one another.

We force ourselves to move again, plant a flower
to hold us here, wonder what we'd call back from a love so brief.
We split apart, lamb and mother driven to the slaughter.

What next? we ask once more.
What lasts will not be shorn by grief.
Our losses fall in love with one another.
Though torn apart, we are both lamb and mother.

ALL THE WAY HOME THROUGH THE DARK

They must be the gypsies of the species—those oily starlings moving from one neighborhood to another, from sycamore to maple in search of friendly limbs to spend a scattered night on. Always they surprise. Suddenly, just there. Like the evening I stopped for a traffic light in front of the hospital one of those mild winter days, forsythia bursting to bloom, December coaxing everything into believing again. There beside the diseased photinia lining the parking lot, their voices settling deep into the spotted leaves, I rolled the window down, wanting to listen hard. I didn't want the light to change. Then a bearded man came down the walk, carrying his cardboard bed folded beneath his arm. And he stopped, too. Just as the light turned to caution, he clapped his hands and laughed. The birds flurried; the leaves shook amid the clatter. He clapped again and laughed, orchestrating their dark rapture. And then the light was green. Something hovered like wings. But a driver honked, so my life moved on. All the way home through the dark, I wanted to sing the gypsies' song.

RUTH

I was drawn to her by the colored
illustration in the *Bible for Young Folks*
my mother gave me when I turned ten.
Sunday evenings, while Brother Hodges
pounded the pulpit, I leaned against
Mama's shoulder and tried to stay awake,
softly turning the pages until they opened to

  Ruth in the ripened fields
  gleaning the ears of corn.

So many times I imagined myself
beside her, bare feet burning on hot soil
the way Mama said hers did when she worked
the cotton rows in Georgia.

I pictured Ruth's hair silky golden
in the sun. And the corn stalks blazed
the day she first saw Boaz.

I had it all wrong, of course.
For when I read her words

  *Whither thou goest,
  I will go...*

I thought she made that vow
to him. I heard her voice—mysterious,
melodious—whisper to Boaz
when he awakened near a heap of corn
and found her lying at his feet.

Some Sundays after Mama shook
the preacher's hand, she led me across
Beaver Street to the doughnut shop
where I spun dreams, whirling 'round
and 'round on the counter stool,
thinking of Ruth—
how she stayed so pretty and clean,
dressed in blue, a yellow silken
scarf. And
how it happened that

she just switched gods,
forsook her folk for others.

In my mind Ruth worked always
close to the edge of the field,
glancing up, ready to abandon
everything if Boaz beckoned.

would Mama ever do that?
I wondered.

It would be years before
the answer came.
But many nights she took my hand
and we walked silently
down the cracked sidewalk
past Abdoulah's Grocery
into the dark,
wooded street
we followed home.

BERNSTEIN

The morning I heard
Bernstein had died
I was driving to class
down Independence,
listening to WDAV,
when the news spun
me back to the '50s
where I was vacuuming
the living room rug,
proud that I had a job
and could afford to join
the Record of the Month
Club. I'd ordered
Gershwin and Beethoven
and Chopin,
having been swept away
by Liberace's pianistics,
his "most requested"
Canadian Sunset and
the *Warsaw Concerto.*

It was the summer
of my first paycheck.
I'd bought a brand new
RCA Victrola
and turned it up
so loud
the music soared above
the whine
of the Sears motor.
It was a summer
of Hungarian fantasies,
swollen kisses
and polonaises—
the summer I graduated
from drive-in movies
to the balcony
of the downtown
Ritz.
It was the summer
I dreamed Indian love calls
and wrote letters in the sand

with my big toe
and hid behind the menu
at the Green Pig Diner
when the juke box played
Smoke
    Gets
        in
            Your
                Eyes.
It was the summer
of moonlight sonatas
and *Malagueña.*

But the morning
Gershwin's *Rhapsody in Blue*
entered my heart,
I turned the cleaner off
and sat still
in the platform rocker,
eyes closed, picturing
Bernstein at the piano
conducting
the New York Philharmonic;
imagined me on the front row
of the concert hall,
wearing white gloves
and applauding for an encore.
Again
and
again,
I
put
the
needle
down.

INVENTORY

We were taking inventory that morning.
I'd listed my pencils and crayons,
blue writing tablets, rulers, erasers,
the balled-up paper I'd shoved
into the darkest corner of my desk.
I almost included the wad of Bazooka
some third grader before me had stuck
inside the inkwell, but I didn't dare, intimidated
by Mrs. Glass's glare and afraid she'd scold
and drag me to the cloakroom,
though something compelled me
to add the practice test I'd seen blowing
across someone's lawn on my way to school.
It just kept showing up inside my head.
"That doesn't belong there!" Mrs. Glass snapped,
brandishing her red pencil and writing a **-1**
across the top of my inventory.

Just the other night I recalled it
when the DJ announced:
"This is *not* an emergency.
It is only a practice warning!"
And the shrill whine of a thousand
mosquitoes pierced my ear drums
with Mrs. Glass's name
and I saw that practice test
snagged in fescue,
teased by the wind,
and felt her hand
snatch my list and brand again
that red **-1** on my mind.

MAP
for L

Draw me a map of your world.
Show the way the harvest moon
rose warped one September
over the barn in the meadow.
Place the chestnuts on the blanket
where you lay summer nights
parading gingerbread boys
across the moon. Don't forget
to place the pond in the field
and show me how you tied Ken
and Barbie to the fishing line
and cast them into the water,
then rescued them and pressed
their wet bodies together
when you thought you knew
what *sex* could do. Leave
that scene and draw
your grandmother tending
the fire, your grandfather carving
a walking stick from red maple.
Invent what you need to make
the valleys deep and rolling.
Don't be afraid to draw
the river where you almost drowned
and the tree that lightning struck,
killing eight cows sheltering beneath it.
And show me where the church
stood that morning when you dressed
in black patent-leather shoes
and fastened your bracelet
before you frowned into the camera.
You *always* frowned, you tell me.
Put that on the map, too.
The scoldings.

THE PATH TO ALLIGATOR POND
for my nephew

                       It's the fourth of July,
and my brother is shaking charcoal briquettes
into the rusty grill, preparing for the neighborhood
cookout. My nephew leans against my car and teases
me about living in Charlotte, the "preppie" town,
he calls it, where in all the summers he's visited
he's never noticed anyone spit tobacco
onto the sidewalk or drive around in a beat-up
low rider.

                          He has exploded
into adolescence and towers over me in his black
House of Pain T-shirt.
Two trailers down from where we're standing,
the police are kicking in the door
to rescue a girl who has O.D.'d on crack.
When I caution him to be careful, he reminds me
he's no longer a kid.
                           The summer he turned
ten, we celebrated at Carowinds.
All day he limped on sore feet, but begged to stay
for just one more ride.
                       A few years later
his mother called long distance, telling me
he had run away from Yulee, back to Jacksonville.
He walked twenty-one miles along I-95
with trucks whipping past and blisters burning.
                          He found his way,
following white lines,
exit ramps,
Waffle House lights;
back to Dunn Avenue,
to a section called Polly Town,
to the father he keeps trying not to lose.

                         Earlier this morning
he asked if I'd walk down the path
to Alligator Pond.

"No, thanks," I laughed. "Just saw a special on
alligators. They cut across land *pretty* fast!"
"Zigzag," he answered. "Just run zigzag.
They won't catch you." Shifting his feet now
he says, "I just don't get it, Aunt Irene.
You go dog sledding and hike where wolves
run loose, but you're afraid to ride the Vortex
at Carowinds or walk to Alligator Pond."
He lives on the edge. I am drawn to it.
I think of his instructions for the cookout:
"Remember, the neighbors carry guns.
They're a nice bunch. Just don't meet their eyes
when you walk by. Look down at the ground.
You'll be fine."
I glance at the thick woods bordering the dirt road
behind the trailers.

                       Right now it seems
his biggest fear is that he'll flunk the G.E.D.
because he can't "*properly* punctuate
a two-hundred-word essay."
He emphasizes *properly*, stroking his chin,
his brown eyes streetwise, watching the road
the way a fox would—fired by the sun—
or like a buck suddenly turning in a clearing.

                       I don't lecture.
Or preach. Or attempt to tame the poet in him
with a lesson on comma splices.
I even resist the urge to say how my heart skips
when he reveals his secret dream
to get a driver's license and a job
so he can start saving to build an underground
nightclub for kids under eighteen.
"West side's already lost," he says.
"The north side needs one. It'll be clean.
A place to hang out, get off the streets.
No drugs. I've even got a name for it: 'The Jungle.'"
"Can I visit when I come to town?"
"Sure. It'll have a bouncer. I'll tell him,
'You let her in free. That's my aunt.'"

LEAVING, ANOTHER SUMMER
for Lorie

Standing at the cabin door
beneath yellow porch light,
I cast a two-toned shadow
into the pre-dawn hour.
My breath forms a thin white trail
vanishing.
Hard to say what is coming,
what is leaving.
The oaks tremble, and the air
hints of rain.
I watch the red lights of the car
disappear behind the curve, surprised
by how long I can hear the tires
grinding into gravel.
I think of you in the back seat,
curled into fantasy the way I did
at your age, longing for home yet
bearing the early weight of goodbyes.
I imagine you will sleep all the way
to Savannah to keep from crying.
The car, no doubt, has moved
onto the highway and is whirring
through the fog down 181 towards
Morganton. I welcome the sweet tap
of rain on the roof, half-dreaming
of the raccoon we saw last night
parting the wind-filled darkness.

IT IS SNOWING IN BELFAST, MAINE
for my brother, Ralph

I look up into the blue dome of midnight
as we walk the hushed streets of this village,

magi to one another, bestowing gifts no one else can.
In the sudden whiteness of a burst of snow,

the swell of our childhood melds into the New Year.
I watch the flakes settle onto his broad shoulders,

watch our shadows stretch to meet the slant of hill
before our boots press against where we have been.

A slow wind sifts the snow into our tracks,
and all is white once more, the going slower,

my knee throbbing in the nine-degree cold.
We stop before a weathered house, each window

warmed by candles. I am drawn to the yellow glow
of those rooms—as if we once had lived there—

and to the wrinkled felt snowman someone
has tacked to the kitchen door.

Blue lights on a small pine beside the porch
blink sleepily. "It's the blue ones that take me home,"

I say. He nods, but doesn't say it—
that being his way.

We stamp the cold and linger,
our thoughts somewhere in the darkness

behind those blue lights, the faint
rumble of a train calling us back.

STROUPIE, ONE AUTUMN

My mountain friend keeps hearing birds call her name.
She swears she heard them in the woods this morning
when dawn rose behind her cabin. And last summer
—through her broken windshield—
she thought she could identify that bird.
I don't say what I'm thinking because it scares me
and might frighten her, although she's said the only
thing she's ever feared is fire.
   I could walk through Death's door right now,
she told me yesterday, cutting a path through the air
with her hands. I wonder if we all will hear
some special call. I've read of the patterns observed
in the dreams of the dying: trees with one side leafless.

THE TRAIN MAN

1.

I don't know where he came from—
the black man who pulled his wooden wagon
through the streets of Jacksonville,

his hands gripping the boards that braced the load,
elbows pointed outward, shoulders locked
to balance the cart on two wheels.

He was almost trotting the first time I saw him.
Mama and I were walking door to door
in a neighborhood I'd never seen before,

delivering **Vote for Me** leaflets for the sheriff.
The sun was a throbbing blister on the sky.
I was squinting at squiggly lines of heat

rising from the sidewalks, trying to decide
whether I'd get a grape or a banana Popsicle
at lunchtime, when I glanced up and saw him

turning the corner. Mama took my hand and said:
  "That man was struck by a train
    and, ever since, he thinks he's one."

Stuffed with old rags and bottles and broken
chairs, the cart looked like a portable dump.
Rusting cans, tied to the back, clattered and scraped.

I wondered if he thought he was the engineer
or the engine, puffing and steaming across town,
pulling the boxcar of his life.

2.

The next time I spotted the Train Man
I was riding the bus. It was payday.
Mama had paid the bills at City Hall and bought

me a red windmill at Kress's 5 & 10
and herself a small parchment bag of roasted cashews.
Holding my windmill out the window,

I grew impatient for the bus to pick up speed
as it strained to climb the viaduct that separated
downtown from where we lived.

Crossing over—going or coming—was always an adventure.
Today my heels had clicked and echoed when I skipped
across the marble floors at City Hall.

I'd spent my nickel on a Payday candy bar
from the blind man who wore black glasses
and whose cane tapped solemn notes through the hallways.

But now thick exhaust fumes were filling my nose
as the bus lumbered to the top of the viaduct,
leaving my windmill motionless.

Looking down and through the spaces between
the concrete railings, I could see people milling around
the produce stands of the Beaver Street Fruit Market.

When the bus began its descent, I caught a glimpse
of Train Man rummaging through some flimsy crates,
probably foraging for bruised oranges or cabbages

for his next railroad run.

3.

The last time I saw Train Man
was from the back seat of the green Plymouth.
Mama was driving my brothers and me to Blackshear

to visit Grandma. The window was down,
and I was caught up in the whine of tires over tar
and the magic of tall pines blurring fast.

I kept an eye out for Burma Shave signs,
not wanting to miss a word.
Now and then I recited little poems to the wind.

All of a sudden—but as if in slow motion—
we passed him. I could have touched his cart.
He was chugging along the side of Highway 23

on a boiler of a day, sweat streaming from his face,
wearing a sweater and a red hat with a jingle bell
that dangled from the tip—something like an elf

would wear at Christmas. He beamed and jerked
one arm as though he were pulling a train's whistle.
I figured the bell was to warn people the train was passing.

4.

                        I remember days
when I hoped the bus would not make its stops
because I wanted to keep riding so I could see

everything all over again, though I knew some things
would have already changed:

> The woman who had been nursing her baby
> on a front porch would be inside the
> shotgun house, boiling turnip greens
> and rutabagas for supper.
>
> A man that was standing at the curb on McDuff,
> tapping tobacco onto a cigarette paper,
> would have finished his smoke, walked
> into Pony's Bar and blown his paycheck.
>
> Waiting on the doorsteps at home, his wife
> would begin crying when the bus rolled past
> one more time without stopping.
>
> And Train Man
>   lost in his tracks
>   would have vanished.

HOW CAN I STOOP TO WASH MY FACE IN THE SURPRISE?
for my brother—an unsent pantoum

Today I imagine the wind scattering your ashes
across the baseball field at Woodstock Park.
How, then, can I stoop to wash my face in the surprise
of blackberry blossoms white above the rosy dianthus?

Across the baseball field at Woodstock Park
you ran from center field, threw the ball like a hot star
of blackberry blossoms white above the rosy dianthus.
I wonder how many springs

you ran from center field, threw the ball like a hot star.
On the vacant lot beside our house
I wonder how many springs
I pitched it burning into your glove.

On the vacant lot beside our house,
training you not to flinch,
I pitched it burning into your glove.
Now in your forty-seventh spring, you buy a cap for the balding.

Training you not to flinch
the radiologist beams a light into your body.
In your forty-seventh spring, you buy a cap for the balding.
You lie on the table, center field, eyes squinting.

The radiologist beams a light into your body.
Each X-mark on your chest becomes a glove.
You lie on the table, center field, eyes squinting.
You catch every ray. Smile when you leave, adjusting the cap.

Each X-mark on your chest becomes a glove.
How, then, can I stoop to wash my face in the surprise?
You catch every ray. Smile when you leave, adjusting the cap.
And today I imagine the wind scattering your ashes.

2584

for my brothers

Lord have mercy! Come on in. You kids look just like your mama and daddy. Got his hair. You don't remember me, I bet, but I watched you many a time walkin' down the sidewalk on the way to school. Brother Hodges says you'd like to walk through the house. That's fine. We bought it after your folks divorced, you know. Make yourselves at home now. That picture hangin' on the wall over the sofa used to be your mama's. Oh! You *do* remember it? Well, your dear mama, bless her poor soul, sold it to me. It came with the house. Go on into the bedrooms and look around. This sure was a little house for all of you. We've often wondered where you all slept. . . . That black and white tile on the bathroom floor is the original. . . . Oh! You remember that, too? Some plumber asked about it once. Said it sure was in good shape and he wondered if it was here when your daddy bought the house—when was it? '39? Yep, these are the original hardwood floors. I had the carpets taken up. Sanded the wood down myself. It's a sturdy house. Not a rotten board anywhere. Your daddy kept it up real nice. Come on into the kitchen. There's a knick-knack in there that belonged to your mama. I bought it, too. Yep. Hangin' up on the wall—that green fryin' pan with the red cherries in the center. It's right cute, ain't it? I want y'all to know now that I've got a note in your mama's handwritin' stating that I bought this fryin' pan *and* that picture over the sofa from her. It's attached to the deed. You know, she wasn't in her right mind when the house sold. One morning she came down to my house over on Orchard and said she had a pot she needed to sell. And do you know that by the time I could get myself dressed proper and haul-buggied over here to buy it, she'd done up and sold *my* pot to Mrs. Hodges! Look up there. That's the original chandelier hangin' over the dining room table. Did y'all eat in here? . . . No, I don't know whatever happened to the maple bookcase. Deacon Akers told me at Wednesday night's prayer meetin' that Irene'd been askin' around about it—said your mama gave it to you for—what was it? your high school graduation? Well, for a long time some of the furniture was stored down on the corner in Myrtle's house. But Myrtle's dead and gone now. Your mama's cedar chest was down there the longest while. Too bad you was away in college when it all happened. You mighta got somethin' if you'd been around. By the way, did your mama ever drink anything besides . . . wine? . . . . No, I'm not interested in selling the picture over the sofa. I right like it. Sure, I'll contact you if I ever change my mind. Your mama shore kept you dressed nice. Looked like you stepped outta a band wagon. Well, come back when you're in town again. Anytime.

MEDITATION IN JANUARY

Insomnia at three,
sweet jazz oozing
through the radio,
and I'm lying here
reading the mystics—
how in touch
with simple things—
Julian of Norwich
finding her world
in a hazelnut;
Blake, his grain
of sand.

———

    Autumn in New York
and I wonder where you are
    Take the A Train
and I think how pain has changed
    My Foolish Heart
no longer acute or piercing
like
that sax note of longing
just
smooth over bone
so much a part of me
that
when I stop
to listen
    Blue and Sentimental
the pure sweet note
hums.

———

By dawn
the Greek
neighbor's
rooster
is crowing
and the rain
has turned
to snow.
I go out
with my dog
to greet it.
How gently
it falls,
easing
the senses.
The dog,
exhilarated,
chases
the snowballs
I toss,
bites,
then shakes
ice
from his teeth.

———

    For a moment
standing amid the soft wet
silence   of snow
        falling
I feast   on the
curve of twigs
    curled like fingers
               from the branches
of the cherry tree   each braced

to catch the   weight of snow
     and hold with
infinite grace
        what settles there

STONE OFFERINGS
for Sheryl

Climbing Bear Mountain, I add my rocks to the cairns along the trail, one, a stone for a friend whose husband, on dialysis for two years, must now have both legs amputated. "Celebrate your independence!" she wrote, telling me how on the fourth of July she strolled him in his wheelchair through the streets of Charleston. Their little girl asked: "Mommy, will you live a long time?" And then, "Will Daddy?"

I drink from my water bottle, raise my arm in a show of strength as my companion photographs me near the peak. *Feeling too good to have something seriously wrong,* I'm thinking, unable to shed the memory of ultra-sounds, the CAT scan, and the upcoming procedure. "Ruling out," the doctor calls it. I continue the climb, recall hiking alone one summer in Mendocino and taking a photo of my Vasque boots and knapsack.

And another summer. In Assisi, noticing my shoes reflected in the mirror at a sidewalk sale, I photographed that image, thinking *that* would be my self-portrait. On my early morning pilgrimage to The Hermitage where St. Francis had often retreated to his cave, the church bells echoed across the city, molten in the sun that rose to the path.

I crawled into the cave of one of his disciples. Someone had placed a white candle in a hollow place of the rock wall. A small mound of stone offerings, to which I added one, rested on the dusty floor. Curled inside the cave I felt pressed. I did not know what to pray, and in haste asked for strength for the unknown and for my legs to carry me— always. It seemed too bold, so I altered it: *and should that fail?* I asked. Then, what? Courage? Grace? I know I left unsatisfied.

ON MEISTER CLIMBING THE FENCE IN SPRING
after Richard Eberhart

It is what he does not know,
climbing the fence in Spring
that troubles me, not him.
It is what he does not know
of cherry blossoms on the ground
and the white hyacinth's resurrection.
It is what he does not know
about cataracts, ozone layers, and acid
rain and his own chemistry
that wins my praise
and makes me laugh when he laps
from the bird bath and sprints
across the lawn after a grackle
that just lighted.
But when he chases a rabbit
with few places to hide,
that troubles me, not him.
He slips behind the hedge
and glances back to see if I am watching
before he climbs the wire and balances
on the split-rail poised for the leap.
It is that he does not know why
I'm shouting, "Down!"
or what has happened to
the black bear that wandered down the mountain
that troubles me. When he escapes
into a neighbor's world, it is what
he does not know about No Trespassing
and rush hours and tires that screech
that frightens me.
It is what he does not know
of Shakespeare, Picasso, Verdi
and Princess Diana
and of this risky business of
writing poetry
and what it's like to lose one's nerve.
And because he *is* what I do not know
I applaud his defiance,
this bundle of energy I think I own—
this magnificent little Houdini.

THE POEM MIGHT BEGIN WITH MORNINGS

faces at windows
 blurred in morning rain

crisp whispers

from a white uniform
  when the nurse enters the room
    unannounced

and it will grow still
  in a monotoned hush of
    secrets, physicians
      flipping through charts,
telling us *hearing*
        is the last sense to go,
as if the father lying there
  could not hear *that.*

The poem will speak of water:
  crushed ice in a spoon tilted
    between parched lips;
and water of memory—lakes looping
 around cypress stumps that suck
   eternal motion deep into their roots.

It will hold something of the
  joy he took in the struggle
    of a rainbow on the line,
patience at the still moment
 of release from the hook,

his marveling at the gills opening
  like valves in the bottom
    of the boat, pleasure
      in slickness of bass
        in glint of knife
        that sent scales
        flying towards the sun.

It will include
 the surprise questions

   was I a good father?

that floated in and out

   when did your mother die?

of comas

   what time did I die?

how he turned to you and said

   find a pencil in the drawer and
   write whatever I say in my sleep. . .
   about setting the traps for quail in the woods
   and hunting squirrel at Brandy Branch . . .
   jot it down if it means anything to you . . .

So it will concern itself with final dreams:
 how he dreamed the funeral,
  named which friends were there.

And the moon, too—how it broke
 through the blinds
  just as you closed his eyes.

Notes

Dedication Page:
The quote is from a poem, "2584," which my brother Ralph wrote to me for Thanksgiving 1991.

Page 6:
"The Escape, Honolulu": Tyke, a circus elephant, began showing signs of psychological distress as early as 1988, yet remained on the circus circuit until 1994 when she killed her trainer at a circus performance in Honolulu and fled through the downtown area where she was gunned down. (*Mainstream*, Winter 1997)

Page 19:
"Steep Ravine" is for Monica Diebold.

Page 38:
The museum referred to in "On the Museum Wall at Terezín, a Handkerchief" is the Museum of the Terezín Ghetto, which was established in October 1991. Between 1941-45, 140,000 Jews were transported to Terezín from all over Europe. More than 33,000 Jews died there. Out of the 87,000 who were transported to extermination camps in Poland, mostly Auschwitz, "less than 4,000 survived . . . victims included . . . thousands of children who left behind nothing but drawings that became for the whole world a symbol of monstrosity of the 'Final Solution.'" The Museum serves both to document the tragic history and to memorialize the victims. See *Museum of the Terezín Ghetto*, trans. Gita Zbavitelová (OSWALD for Památnik Terezín, 1992).

Page 48:
"One World": The line, "our losses fall in love with one another," came to me in a dream.

Back Cover:
Wordsworth's "spots of time" alluded to in Peter Meinke's comments are from Wordsworth's long autobiographical work, *The Prelude*, Book XII, a portion of which follows:

> There are in our existence spots of time,
> That with distinct pre-eminence retain
> A renovating virtue, whence, depressed
> By false opinion and contentious thought,
> Or aught of heavier or more deadly weight,
> In trivial occupations, and the round
> Of ordinary intercourse, our minds
> Are nourished and invisibly repaired;
> . . . Such moments
> Are scattered everywhere, taking their date
> From our first childhood.

ABOUT THE AUTHOR

Irene Blair Honeycutt grew up in Jacksonville, Florida and has lived in South Carolina, Illinois, and Tennessee. She now lives in Charlotte, NC, and teaches creative writing at Central Piedmont Community College where she is the director of the college's Annual Spring Literary Festival. She also teaches journal writing at Queens College and leads writing workshops around the region. In addition, her interests in mythology and classic fairy tales have led her to teach classes through the Haden Institute in Charlotte.

Honeycutt's first poetry manuscript, *It Comes as a Dark Surprise*, won Sandstone Publishing's Regional Poetry Contest in 1992 and underwent four printings. Her poems have won awards and have appeared in national journals, including *Nimrod, Asheville Poetry Review, Cold Mountain Review, Southern Poetry Review, Pembroke Magazine, Devil's Millhopper, Croton Review, Crucible, The Arts Journal,* and *St. Andrews Review*.

She has also seen her poems anthologized in *Sandburg-Livesay International Award Anthology, Only Morning in Her Shoes* (Utah State University Press); *Trapping Time Between the Branches, No Hiding Place: Uncovering the Legacy of Charlotte Area Writers,* and most recently in *Earth and Soul* in which all poems were translated into Russian and widely distributed in Russia.

In 1998 *Creative Loafing* magazine acknowledged Honeycutt by giving her the Best of Charlotte Award for the Best Contribution to the Improvement of the Literary Climate in the city of Charlotte. In 1997 the Charlotte Writers Club honored her by naming her the first recipient of the Adelia Kimball Founders Award because of her advocacy for writers.

Honeycutt received her M.A. degree in English from East Tennessee State University. She has studied at Bread Loaf in Vermont; at the Art of the Wild Writers Workshop in Squaw Valley, CA. She received a North Carolina Arts Council Scholarship to study at the Prague Summer Writers Workshop in the Czech Republic. In 2000 Honeycutt became the recipient of a Creative Fellowship from the Arts and Science Council.

NOVELLO festival PRESS

Novello Festival Press, under the auspices of the Public Library of Charlotte and Mecklenburg County, will, through the publication of books of literary excellence, enhance the awareness of the literary arts, help discover and nurture new literary talent, celebrate the rich diversity of the human experience, and expand the opportunities for writers and readers from within our community and its surrounding geographic region.

About The Public Library of Charlotte and Mecklenburg County

For more than a century, The Public Library of Charlotte and Mecklenburg County has provided essential community service and outreach to the citizens of the Charlotte area. Today, it is one of the premier libraries in the country—named "Library of the Year" and "Library of the Future" in the 1990s—with 23 branches; 1.6 million volumes; 20,000 videos and DVDs; 9,000 maps and 8,000 compact discs. The Library also sponsors a number of community-based programs—from the award-winning Novello Festival of Reading, a celebration that accentuates the fun of reading and learning—to its branch programs for young people and adults.